The Jesus Diet
How the Holy Spirit Coached Me to a 50-Pound Weight Loss

Robin Merrill

ISBN-10:0991270606
ISBN-13:978-0-9912706-0-6

Edited by Laura Jones

Cover Design by Priscilla Pantin

Welcome

My weight loss journey began when I nailed my fat to the cross.

I was at SoulFest, an annual Christian music festival in the mountains of New Hampshire. There I was, pressed up against the stage, worshipping in the hot sun, and a thought occurred to me.

You don't have to be a slave to food. You can be healthy. This story isn't over.

Where on earth did *that* come from? Hmm. I wonder. Probably not from anywhere on earth.

A wooden cross stood near the stage. A bucket of nails and a hammer sat at the bottom of the cross. Later that day, I said a prayer as I pounded a nail into the cross: "Lord, please set me free from my addiction to food. I want to be healthy for you." I didn't fully understand what I was doing, but I knew it was serious. I knew that something was happening as I pounded that nail into the wood.

You see, I had, and still struggle with, an unhealthy relationship with food. I was a slave to it. I overate. I emotionally ate. I was unhealthy.

Today, I am much healthier. By the power of God, I have lost 50 pounds.

I wrote this book to a specific audience: my sisters and brothers who also struggle with food. If you do not fall under this generalization, by all means, you are still welcome to join us. If you do, however, fall under this generalization, know that I'm right there with you.

Anytime I challenge you to do something differently, to be vulnerable, to surrender, I am also challenging myself to the same. This isn't some skinny-mini preaching to you about carrot sticks. If you have ever battled a peanut butter cup, you and I are kindred spirits. And if you want to lose weight, then I want to help you. I want to share a few of the things God has taught me along my journey.

> Blessed be the God and Father of our Lord Jesus Christ, the Father of mercies and God of all comfort, who comforts us in all our affliction so that we will be able to comfort those who are in any affliction with the comfort with which we ourselves are comforted by God. (2 Corinthians 1:3–4)

Warning: I Am Going to Spiritualize Weight Loss

> For our struggle is not against flesh and blood, but against the rulers, against the powers, against the world forces of this darkness, against the spiritual forces of wickedness in the heavenly places. (Ephesians 6:12)

I've been told by many admirable Christians not to "over-spiritualize." I'm not trying to over-spiritualize, I promise. But here's the thing: I tried every diet, read every health book, and subscribed to every new eating philosophy. Nothing worked. Until I recognized that my physical health depended fully on my spiritual health.

I had to declare war on my fat.

I'd been seriously overweight since my first pregnancy, but I never took it seriously. I saw it as no big deal. I made excuses. I rationalized. I had much more important things to worry about. But as long as I kept my poor health "no big deal," I was unable to do anything about it.

When I declared war on my fat, it became a very big deal very quickly.

When I declared war on my fat, forces seemed to come out of nowhere to stop me. I had overwhelming physical cravings. People who were close to me, people who had tremendous influence on my life, tried to convince me that my weight was no big deal. Friends and family members encouraged me to overeat and to eat unhealthy foods. I felt like I had stepped into the Twilight Zone, but I hadn't. It was just that were spiritual forces at work.

Once I realized that, I recognized that I had to fight back.

 When I began to fight back, when I made my health a big deal, when I declared war on my fat, God was right there to help me win the war.

I used to coach softball, and I used to tell my players, "90 percent of a softball game happens in your head." For me, 90 percent of the weight loss process happened in my heart. For me, weight loss was incredibly spiritual.

Prayer:

Heavenly Father, please make me aware of the spiritual elements of my physical health. Please arm me with the spiritual weapons I need to win this battle for my health. Thank you for giving me the power to win. Amen.

No Condemnation

> Therefore there is now no condemnation for those
> who are in Christ Jesus. (Romans 8:1)

There is no condemnation for those who are in Jesus. Isn't that the best news you've ever heard? If you have trusted Jesus as your personal Savior, there is no condemnation for you. You have been found not guilty. You will not be condemned. You will not die for your sins.

This is true on the big scale. It is also true on the small scale.

If you struggle with weight, chances are you've experienced some condemnation from the world. You've probably also experienced some condemnation from yourself. Listen. The world's condemnation should mean nothing to you. You are in Jesus. You are not in this world. Who cares what the world thinks? Block it out. Care what Jesus thinks. If you are condemning, yourself, cut it out! There is no condemnation for you.

When you condemn yourself, you are essentially saying that the work of the cross wasn't enough. It was enough. It was enough to cover every mistake you've ever made. You are free from condemnation. You are free.

When I decided to make a change, I asked my doctor for help. I knew how to lose weight in theory, but I wanted to ask for a professional opinion. My doctor gave me lots of advice, but one of the most important things she said to me was, "Stop being so hard on yourself. You have not ruined your life. You've just gotten into a bit of trouble and now you need to get out of it."

Framing my challenge this way made it seem hopeful. I had just gotten myself into a little bit of trouble. God would get me out of it just as he always does.

Many of us are overweight *because* we are so hard on ourselves. Our self-condemnation, low self-esteem, and abusive eating patterns are often intricately related. I *had* to stop condemning myself in order to make room for the freedom Jesus was offering.

Prayer:

Jesus, thank you for freeing me from condemnation. Please forgive me for condemning myself and help me to stop doing that. Please help me to walk in the freedom you died to make possible. Thank you, Savior. Amen.

The Jesus Diet

> Now those who belong to Christ Jesus have crucified the flesh with its passions and desires. (Galatians 5:24)

Every diet I ever tried promised me something along these lines: "This isn't a diet. It's a lifestyle."

Horse feathers! This, my friends, is a diet. And it is an honor to call it so.

Why? Because in order to become healthier, our fleshly desires must *die*. We must crucify them.

When I gave my life to Jesus, my spirit came to life. But my flesh (my own selfish desires) was still right there. The flesh, the person I was, didn't automatically disappear. In fact, to get rid of her, I have to *work* at it. Romans 8:13 calls it "putting to death the deeds of the body."

The secret to the Jesus diet is Jesus. The secret is the cross. When we crucify ourselves, when we die at the foot of the cross, our real life begins—*our freedom begins.*

But the Jesus diet starts with dying. Anything, everything worth living for, *must* start with the death of our flesh. The grain of wheat *must* fall into the ground and die if it is ever going to live, if it is ever going to be productive for Jesus (John 12:24; 1 Corinthians 15: 36).

How do we do such a thing? This whole idea can seem mighty foreign to us practical folks. I had to get on my knees. I had to fall down before my God, before his cross, and ask him to take my life. Then, I had to continually give it up. In every moment, in the face of each temptation, I had to continually beg him to kill my flesh and its wants. I knew it was the only way I could live.

Jesus is calling you right now. He's inviting you to the life he has planned for you. He's inviting you to the cross, where you will die, and where you will find life.

Prayer:

Heavenly Father, thank you for this opportunity. Please help me learn to do a better job of killing my selfish and self-destructive desires. Please make me healthy. Please help me to lose weight. Please empower me with your Spirit. Amen.

The Only Teacher You Need

> As for you, the anointing which you received from Him abides in you, and you have no need for anyone to teach you; but as his anointing teaches you about all things, and is true and is not a lie, and just as it has taught you, you abide in Him. (1 John 2:27)

I recently took a box of books to a used book store. The kind man behind the counter picked out the Stephen King books and the Loretta Lynn biography and slid the remaining diet books back across the counter. "Sorry, these don't sell."

I was startled. Seriously? I thought everybody bought diet books. Well, many do, but they buy the *new* diet books. They don't want to invest in a dusty old diet that has already failed millions of people. They want to buy the shiny new diet that promises instant deliverance. There is no home for used diet books. How sad for them.

I have had a lot of teachers over the years and their voices have combined in my head, a cacophony of contradictions. And that's too bad, because my Bible clearly tells me that I don't need anyone else to teach me. The Holy Spirit is my teacher.

Now, God certainly provides us with counselors and friends who can encourage us, rebuke us, and help us along the way. But if any voice contradicts the voice of the Holy Spirit, then we need to shut it out. It's not the voice of truth.

Today, the Bible is my only diet book. It's the only one that hasn't failed me. And the Holy Spirit is hands down the best teacher I've ever had. He's caring, loving, patient, and always available for extra help after hours.

Prayer:

Heavenly Father, thank you for the gift of the Holy Spirit. Please help me to be a good student. Please help me to discern between the voices of this world and the voice of the Holy Spirit. Thank you, Father for this journey. Amen.

Holy Spirit as Coach

> But the Helper, the Holy Spirit, whom the Father will send in My name, He will teach you all things, and bring to your remembrance all that I said to you. (John 14:26)

Once upon a time, I hired a health coach. It was a cool experience, and I am not telling you not to hire a health coach. The right health coach might be just what you need. However, I am encouraging you to first solicit the help of the universe's *best health coach.*

My first health coach was a lovely woman who was kind and knowledgeable. But she was human. Her capacity to care about me and my needs was limited. She wasn't on call round the clock. I couldn't call out to her at two in the morning when I was thinking about ripping into a bag of chocolate chips. She was also expensive. The Holy Spirit is completely free.

Being a coach is not easy. I know, I've spent a lot of time trying. I love coaching and I love my athletes like my own daughters, but my compassion and patience are limited. Want to tap into an unlimited source of compassion and patience? The Holy Spirit is ready. No matter how many times I needed Him to teach me the same thing over and over, he did it.

When I was a humble (and humiliated) mess, he was right there to listen, encourage, and get me back up off the bench. When I was a stubborn, arrogant base runner refusing to recognize the steal sign, he was there to holler, "Run!"

The Holy Spirit continues to be there for me each day, coaching me every step of the way. He adapts to the coaching style I need at any given moment. (If you've never heard one of his locker room pep talks, you are really missing out!) He is a supernatural coach with limitless knowledge and power. I can't imagine why I ever wanted to do this without him.

Prayer:

Father, thank you for giving me the Holy Spirit to coach me through this life. Help me to want to hear his voice. Help me to hear his voice. Help me to obey his voice. Help me to be coachable. I so want to win this battle for you, Father. Thank you. Amen.

It's Not Really about What You Eat

All things are lawful for me, but not all things are profitable. All things are lawful for me, but I will not be mastered by anything. (1 Corinthians 6:12)

I've read the Bible and not found a single verse that says I can't have a slice of pumpkin cheesecake. I have however, found verses that suggest we are not designed to be enslaved by pumpkin cheesecake.

My journey toward health had very little to do with what I ate, and everything to do with the state of my heart while I was eating.

God allows us to eat anything, but we are not to be *mastered* by food. I was, indeed, mastered by food. Operating on my own power, I was powerless against it. I thought about it way too much. I spent way too much money on it. I used it to self-medicate. And I was allowing it to destroy my physical body.

You may respond well to a strict diet full of do's and don't's, but if this isn't your style, don't panic. You don't necessarily have to give up carbs. Or fat. Or everything except cabbage soup.

Instead of starting with the shopping list, start with your heart. Then ask God to help you make decisions, one at a time, about what to put in your shopping cart and what to eventually put in your mouth.

Prayer:

Father, please bring me back to the basics. Please help me depend wholly and solely on you for direction and protection. I don't want to be mastered by anyone or anything other than you. Thank you for your provision. Thank you for seeing into my heart. Please help my heart to honor you in every second of every day. Thank you, Father. Amen.

Faith Is a Gift

> Immediately the boy's father cried out and said, "I do believe; help my unbelief." (Mark 9:24)

Ever feel like you don't have enough faith for all this? Have you ever asked for it?

I did, and what a difference it made!

At one point, long ago, I was really struggling just to believe. It's hard to imagine now, but I didn't yet have the knowledge and experience to back up my faith. I wanted to believe; I felt Jesus calling me, but I just didn't *have* it. I was being tossed about in a sea of doubts.

Then I read this section of Mark. The man wants Jesus to heal his son. I want Jesus to heal me. Jesus says, "All things are possible to him who believes." And the father cries out, "I do believe! Help my unbelief!"

This rang so incredibly true to me. I did believe. I *wanted* to believe. But I had all the pesky doubts. So I asked to be delivered from them. And I was.

Now, please know that it was not done with the flip of a switch. It was a process, one that I am still enjoying, but I am receiving the gift of faith, and I am no longer plagued with doubts.

If you are asking God for the gift of health, but you are having trouble believing for it, ask also for the gift of faith. He will be faithful in honoring your request.

Prayer:

Almighty God, thank you for the gift of faith. Please forgive me when I doubt you. Please forgive me when I doubt your power. I ask you now to erase any unbelief in my heart and replace it with a powerful faith. Thank you, Father! Amen.

God Loves You

> He said, "Take now your son, your only son, whom you love, Isaac, and go to the land of Moriah, and offer him there as a burnt offering on one of the mountains of which I will tell you." (Genesis 22:2)

Chances are that I'm not the first person to tell you that God loves you. I'd been told hundreds of times.

I just didn't believe it.

Then one night, late at night, driving home from a poetry slam that I had lost quite handily, I was listening to "Beautiful" by MercyMe and it hit me.

God loves me.

I had long since accepted that God loves *people*, that God loves *you*, and that God loves *everybody else*, but I had never really accepted the fact that God loves *me*.

To me, "Jesus loved you enough to die on the cross for you" was a worn-out line of doctrine. Jesus died for everyone, right? What did I have to do with it? But there in that car, listening to that song, I realized, *even if I had been the only person on the planet, Jesus still would have died for me.*

It's so hard for us to imagine all of this love and sacrifice on such a supernatural scale. So God gives us the abbreviated study guide in Genesis. God asked Abraham to take his only son to a different land and kill him on a mountain. Could you have done that? I don't think I could have. I don't even like meditating on it long enough to wonder if I could have. Yet

God did. He took his only son, whom he loves, to a different land and killed him on a mountain.

That, my sisters and brothers, is how much God loves *you.* Enough to kill his own son.

It becomes easier for me to value myself, my health, my worth, when I realize that God loves me. *Really* loves me. This isn't just something that we tell our kids in Sunday school. This is a love we can't fathom. Yet we can accept it, and we can allow it to transform us.

People or circumstances in your life may have told you that you are unworthy, unloved, or even unlovable. These are lies from the enemy. The enemy does not want you to know that God loves you. But he does. No matter what you've done, no matter what you look like, no matter what you feel like, God loves you enough to kill his son for you.

> For I am convinced that neither death, nor life, nor angels, nor principalities, nor things present, nor things to come, nor powers, nor height, nor depth, nor any other created thing, will be able to separate us from the love of God, which is in Christ Jesus our Lord. (Romans 8:38–39)

Prayer:

Father, thank you for your unimaginable love. Thank you for loving me enough to send your only son, to offer your only son on the cross. Though I cannot understand this love, help me to accept it. Help me to realize your love even when I feel unlovable. Never let me doubt your love for me ever again. Thank you, Father. Amen.

Temptation

> For since He Himself was tempted in that which He has suffered, he is able to come to the aid of those who are tempted. (Hebrews 2:18)

Listen. You are not in this alone. Just sit with that for a moment.

God loves you. He does not want you to be unhealthy. He does not want you to be unhappy in your own skin.

There are a lot of food temptations in our culture. Giant cheeseburgers on towering billboards. Decadent desserts in glass cases. Pizza commercials during *The Biggest Loser*. Tempting us into overeating is an effective marketing plan.

When you are tempted, know that Jesus was first tempted. He may have not been tempted with French fries and ice cream, but he was certainly tempted. And he is there with you in your temptation. He cares. He wants to help you say no to that temptation and yes to the life he has planned for you.

Call on him! Lean on him! Ask him to carry you through that temptation. He is able, willing, and ready to come to your aid. You just have to want him to. You just have to ask.

Prayer:

Lord Jesus, I thank you that you were tempted. I thank you for standing strong and holy in the face of temptation. Thank you for enabling me to do the same. Help me to remember that I am never alone in any temptation. Thank you, Jesus. Amen.

Sufficient Grace

> And He has said to me, "My grace is sufficient for you, for power is perfected in weakness." Most gladly, therefore, I will rather boast about my weaknesses, so that the power of Christ may dwell in me. (2 Corinthians 12:9)

On a sunny morning in August, I stood upon the very top of Gunstock Mountain in New Hampshire, along with hundreds of other believers. We stood, and we listened, with mouths and hearts dropped open, as a child sang "Your Grace Is Enough" with Matt Maher.

The child was Christopher Duffley, who is blind and autistic. And Christopher has the voice of an angel. He sang every note perfectly. He sang with his physical eyes closed and his spiritual eyes wide open. He sang his heart out to his God. This child who could not see did not stop to mourn the loss of his sight. Instead, he stood there on that mountaintop, in front of the whole world, and he boasted about his weakness. In perfect pitch, that child boasted about the power of Christ that dwells in him. I felt like we were standing very close to heaven that day.

If God's grace is sufficient for that child, if God's grace was sufficient for Paul, then certainly it is sufficient for me.

I do *not* want to stand on a mountaintop and boast to the world about how much I struggle with food. I do *not* want to sing out that I have wept over a pizza. But I should. And here I am, doing it right now: Dear world, I am powerless over food. I crave it. I want it. I eat too much of it. I am unhealthy because of it. And I gladly proclaim this weakness to you now because I know that God will rescue me. I know that in my weakness, he is strong. I know that in my weakness, I am strong in him! I know that his grace is sufficient to deliver me, that his power is made perfect in my weakness. Thank you, Jesus!

Prayer:

Thank you, God, for your grace. Your grace is sufficient for me. I know this. Please remind me of this when I am feeling weak. Please fill me with your strength. Thank you for being strong in my weakness. I praise you for this struggle, for through it, you are drawing me closer to you. Amen.

Anxiety and Food

> Be anxious for nothing, but in everything by prayer and supplication with thanksgiving let your requests be made known to God. (Philippians 4:6)

"Be anxious for nothing."

Just sit with that for a minute. Be anxious ... for *nothing*.

I can't speak for you, but for me, that charge is so daunting, it almost makes me laugh out loud. Anxiety. I hate it. But I come by it naturally. And in order to deal with it, I had to admit it: I was indeed anxious.

I don't like it. I am not proud. In my head, I know God is in control. In my head, I know I can trust him. In my head, I know he will meet my needs and I don't have a thing in the world to be anxious about. But in my heart—well that's a different story. A sadder story.

On many days, my heart is not at peace. On these days, I can feel a physical pressure on my chest. This pressure makes it difficult to breathe. This pressure makes my entire being uncomfortable, uneasy, restless. I can't concentrate. I struggle to be patient and kind with my children.

So I eat. I eat to relax. I eat to calm myself down. I eat to make myself feel better. I eat to kill the anxiety. And it works, for a short time. That serotonin gets flowing and I feel much better. But then I feel guilty. And then that guilt morphs into more anxiety. And then I want to eat more.

26

This behavior is nothing short of absurd. Philippians 4:6 does not say, "Be anxious for nothing, but in everything stuff your face and you will feel better."

Philippians 4:6 tells us to take our anxiety to God in prayer. This is not always easy, but it works. I have tested it time and again and *never* been left wanting. When I say, "God please take this anxiety from me, please lift this pressure from my chest," he does. Now, sometimes he asks me to work through what is causing the anxiety in the moment and this isn't always pleasant, but it is necessary.

Listen: anxiety is a tool of the enemy. Kick it out of your life. Work to replace it with prayer. Make it a habit. Don't let anxiety have its way with you. When anxiety is in control of you, the Holy Spirit isn't.

Prayer:

Lord, please forgive me for feeling anxious. I know Lord that I don't need to feel anxious when I have you. Help me to bring all my concerns to you in prayer. Help me to be thankful in everything. Protect me from anxiety and fill me with your peace. Amen.

Fall in Love with the Bible

> Then I shall not be ashamed
> When I look upon all Your commandments. (Psalm
> 119:6)

Ask me how much I love Psalm 119. I won't answer you. I just don't have the words. This Scripture has changed my very core. It has saved my life over and over again.

I beg you. Read Psalm 119 out loud right now. Do it every morning. Take the time. Make the time. When you are feeling weak. When you are feeling sad. When you are feeling false hunger. When you are feeling anxious. Stop what you are doing and read Psalm 119.

I don't really want to talk about shame in this book. But I do want to be transparent. So here it is: I've wasted a lot of time and energy on shame.

I'm ashamed of mistakes I've made. I'm ashamed of the way I look. I'm ashamed that I can't perform certain physical tasks that a healthy person my age could. The list goes on.

Enough.

I don't want to be ashamed. I want to flip open my Bible and not be ashamed by the words I read. I want to read a verse and say to my God, "Yes, Lord, I am doing that." Or "Yes, God, I will do that." Or at least, "Yes, Jesus, I am trying."

The more I meditated on Psalm 119, the more I fell in love with God's Word, the more I *wanted* to obey God's Word, the easier it became to be obedient, and the further and further shame crept away.

28

God's commandments were not given to limit us, punish us, or control us. They were given to set us free. When I follow God's commandments, the shackles come off and shame is a dress that no longer fits.

Prayer:

Thank you, God, for your Word. Help me to understand it. Help me to write it in my heart. Help me to become obedient to your Word, Lord, to every word of it. Amen.

Fall in Love with the Bible Some More

> Oh, how I love Your law!
> It is my meditation all the day. (Psalm 119:97)

The more time I spend in the Word, the more sense it makes. The more time I spend with it, the more I fall in love.

I grew up in the church. And I was beaten again and again with the *must read your Bible every morning* paddle. I have no desire to thump you with that same paddle.

But I do want to share my testimony with you. And my testimony is this: *on the days when I awoke too busy to spend time in the Word, I almost always ate something I shouldn't have.*

When I woke up and dove into the Word first thing, when I got my heart in the right place before setting my feet on the floor, I almost always got through the day without overeating.

My journey toward good health depended fully on my Bible. I read it. I studied it. I posted snippets of it all over my house (including prominent placements on the fridge and pantry). I listened to it in the car.

On several occasions, when faced with a particularly piercing temptation, I would get up from the table and make a beeline for the Bible. I would open it up and ask that my love for the Bible would wash away my desire for food. And of course, it worked.

All
I saturated my life with God's Word, and the pounds melted
away.

Prayer:

Heavenly Father, thank you for the Bible. Help me to fall
more in love with your Bible every day. Please fill my heart
with a desire for your Word, for your commandments. Please
remind me to go to your Word, every day. Amen.

Say Grace, Every Time

> Rejoice always; pray without ceasing; in everything give thanks; for this is God's will for you in Christ Jesus. (1 Thessalonians 5:16–18)

"How are you doing it?"

That is the question I was asked, over and over. People would notice I was shrinking and would ask me for my secret. The complete answer is a bit too long and involved for passing in the street, so I quickly developed a short version: "I've been praying more."

In my close circle of friends, this resulted in a bit of a joke, "Oh that Robin, she's just praying the weight off."

But it was true.

Here's the thing. I started saying grace *every time I ate anything*.

For example, we are running late this morning. I need to get the kids out the door. There is nothing to eat in the house. They want breakfast. In a moment of panic, I tell them I will get them a donut on the way if they are buckled up in the next ten seconds. They fly out the door. Mission accomplished. I stop to buy them a donut. I'm starving too. I get myself one. But before I take that first bite, I give thanks. I stop. I stop the car. I stop my brain. I stop everything and give thanks for that donut I am about to bite into. And suddenly, I don't want it anymore. The Holy Spirit pipes up loud and clear, "Robin, you do not want that donut."

32

For example, Hubbie leaves an almost empty bag of chips on the counter. I am picking up. I want to throw the bag away. I decide to eat the last five chips. But before I put that first chip to my lips, I say grace. And suddenly, that chip becomes disgusting. Suddenly, I know it needs to go right into the garbage with the bag.

For example, I make a huge salad for my family. A variety of greens, chopped cucumbers, cherry tomatoes, olive oil, and a sprinkling of goji berries. And before I even pick up the fork, I give thanks. And the Holy Spirit says, "You're welcome."

If you want to be healthier, say grace. Every time.

Prayer:

Lord, I thank you and praise you that I can come before you in prayer, that I can approach you with boldness and confidence. Please Lord, remind me to pray. Gently tug on my heart when you know I need to talk to you. Thank you, Lord for providing for me. Thank you for protecting me. Amen.

Strong Arms

> She girds herself with strength
> And makes her arms strong. (Proverbs 31:17)

Land sakes alive, I hope no one is looking at my arms! And yet, here is the Bible, telling us that the ideal woman has great biceps. Hmm. I had better get to work.

Kidding aside, it's pretty obvious that we are created to be physically active. How is this obvious? Because when we are not physically active, we suffer. When we do not exercise, we are more prone to injury and illness. When we do not exercise, we suffer from a lack of energy.

Don't like to exercise? Join the club. But don't let it stop there. Ask God to provide you with a way to exercise in his service. Maybe that's stacking firewood, coaching peewee basketball, playing church softball, or walking an elderly person's dog. I don't know what he's got in store for you, but I do know that when I asked him to help me get busy, he did.

If you have physical injuries and limitations, you *must* work around them. Again, ask God for help. Ask health care professionals how you can get the exercise you need without putting yourself in danger. Ask God the same question.

Then get moving! When I exercise, it is *so* much easier to make smart eating decisions. For starters, I simply feel better and am less tempted to self-medicate. And secondly, if I've invested all that effort in exercise, I'm far less likely to sabotage myself.

So, join me in my quest for strong, Proverbs 31 arms, won't you? (Men, you may want to find a Scripture about Samson's arms if Proverbs 31 isn't doing it for you.)

Prayer:

Heavenly Father, thank you for my physical health. Please make me healthier. Please give me opportunities to exercise. Give me a desire to exercise. Help me to overcome any obstacles. Thank you for carrying me on this journey toward health. Please make me healthier for you. Amen.

Food and Money

> Why do you spend money for what is not bread,
> And your wages for what does not satisfy?
> Listen carefully to Me, and eat what is good,
> And delight yourself in abundance. (Isaiah 55:2)

This is God talking to the Israelites. This is *God* talking. And he is asking me, why do I waste money? Why do I blow it on things of this world, on stuff that *I know* will never satisfy me?

He has a point.

Why *do* I make these foolish decisions? And am I really willing to go down the path to figuring that out? Am I really ready to grow past my habit of physical spending without spiritual consideration?

My relationship with food and my relationship with money are so tightly interwoven, I could not possibly hope to improve one without dealing with the other. And I can't say I was really excited about it. I've never had a God-honoring relationship with either.

That's not to say I'm a criminal. I am honest with my dealings and I've got a great credit score. But I've always seemed to spend just a bit beyond my means. And that continues to get me into trouble.

And where do I spend most foolishly? That's right—on food. When it comes to making spending decisions on food, I tend to let my flesh choose. My stomach chooses to dine luxuriously, on something I can't really afford and don't really need, on something that is not even real bread. These decisions leave my bank account in the red, my spirit unnourished, my God unglorified, and myself unsatisfied. Yet I do it again and again.

I had to start praying before every purchase. Just as I did before every bite.

"Dear God, do I really need to purchase these wood pellets to heat my home? Yes, I do. Thank you, Lord for this provision. Thank you for keeping my family warm and safe."

"Dear God, do I really need to go through this drive-thru? No, I don't. But God, I'm *really* hungry. And it won't cost much. I'll order off the cheap menu. Okay God (sigh), I know you are right. I will keep driving. I will not starve to death if I wait till I get home to eat. Thank you, Lord for your provision and protection."

I'm not saying this is a fun practice. The old me wouldn't have thought twice about that ten dollar donation to America's fast food empire, but the new me, the one God is shaping every day, the one God is shrinking every day, knows that is just foolish.

Food is a tool and God wants me to use it wisely. Money is a tool and God wants me to use it wisely. And these two wisdoms are holding hands tightly.

I am so much happier and healthier when I refuse to spend money on what does not satisfy. I am so much safer when I strive to spend money *only* when that spending will serve God's Kingdom.

Prayer:

Father, help me to make wise decisions with my money. Help me to make decisions that glorify you. Help me to lose weight and become healthier so that I may better serve you. Thank you, Father for your love and guidance. Amen.

Priorities

> But the Lord answered and said to her, "Martha, Martha, you are worried and bothered about so many things; but only one thing is necessary, for Mary has chosen the good part, which shall not be taken away from her." (Luke 10:41–42)

Martha was busy. Mary was just hanging out at Jesus' feet.

I have a busy schedule. Who doesn't? But what is more troublesome to me is the busyness of my mind.

Jesus has asked me to sit at his feet, to listen to his voice, and to do his will. And I have let every conceivable voice distract me:

- *You must finish your meal (and have seconds) or you'll offend the cook.*
- *If you don't clean your plate, you are wasteful and ungrateful. There are starving people all over the world. Oh, and yes, eat your children's leftovers too.*
- *You must partake of the buffet, or people will think you are a snob.*
- *You can't afford a gym membership. That's a waste of money. You're being selfish.*
- *You don't have time to exercise. That will take away from the children.*

Busy, busy, busy. Foolishness. Jesus was asking me to seek him. He was asking me to get healthy for him. And I was prioritizing other things.

I had to seriously rearrange my priorities. And it wasn't easy. It felt like reprogramming my mind. *No, Robin, this is serious. This is your priority right now. Focus. Sit at Jesus' feet and just listen. Listen to his words and obey them. Obey his words only, not the other crazy mutterings running through your busy mind.*

② —

All

I knew that God wanted me to get healthy. For him. For my family. For the Body of Christ. And I had to make that mission my priority, not for myself, but for my God.

③ —

Prayer:

Lord Jesus, help me to get my priorities in order. I want to sit at your feet. I want to live worshipfully. I want to hear your voice, loud and clear. Help me to block out all the sounds that do not come from you. Thank you, dear Jesus. Amen.

A Temple of God

> Do you not know that you are a temple of God and *that* the Spirit of God dwells in you? (1 Corinthians 3:16)

I know you know this verse. We've all been told that our bodies are temples for the Holy Spirit. Have we been told it so often that it has lost its meaning?

I imagine that I have been challenged with decorating a temple for my God. I imagine that many people will see it, that this temple will be a visible, tangible representation of God. I imagine that people will make decisions about God based on what they see in this temple.

So I spare no expense. Making this temple fit for my King is my top priority. Marble floors. Beautiful fountains spouting pure, clean holy water hundreds of feet into the air. Walls trimmed in gold. Scarlet silk curtains. Purple velvet furniture. Aubergine velvet rugs. I would be so proud of this temple. It would feel so good to offer such a temple to my God.

This is not how I treat my body. I do not make the condition of this temple, this non-imaginary temple, a priority. I do spare expense, every day.

I need to change this. I need to make my temple fit for the King. The Holy Spirit lives in me. The bare minimum I can do is give him suitable lodging. I strive to build for him a palace, a palace he will be proud to call his.

Prayer:

Lord Jesus, thank you for the gift of the Holy Spirit. I know that my body is a temple. Please help me to get your temple in order. I want you to be pleased. I want you to be proud of me. I want to be healthy for you. Please help me Jesus. Amen.

Whatever Is True

> Finally, brethren, whatever is true, whatever is honorable, whatever is right, whatever is pure, whatever is lovely, whatever is of good repute, if there is any excellence and if anything worthy of praise, dwell on these things. (Philippians 4:8)

Dwell on these things.

The King James tells us to *think* on these things. The New King James tells us to *meditate* on these things.

We have the mind of Christ (1 Cor. 2:16). We are to take every thought captive for Christ (2 Cor. 10:5).

What we allow our minds to think affects what we allow ourselves to do.

I have the thought, "I really want to go through the drive-thru. I have worked hard today. I deserve to treat myself." Then, because I have the mind of Christ, I recognize (or the Holy Spirit gently points out to me) that these thoughts are not Christ's thoughts. So I take my thoughts captive. I push away the thought of "treating myself" and reach for thoughts about *whatever is true, whatever is honorable, whatever is right* ...

This can be hard. At times, this can feel impossible. It takes practice. I'm still not very good at it, and I've been practicing for a while now.

I have to make time to practice. I have to make time to dwell on these things, so that my brain can do it in the heat of the moment.

I train my brain by feeding it with God's Word. I read it. I listen to it. I train my brain by feeding it with Christian music. It is a lot harder to succumb to the temptation of a drive-thru if Chris Tomlin is belting "No Chains on Me" out of my speakers.

Your mind may work differently than mine, so the details may differ. But we are all instructed to dwell on these good things. Kick out the bad thoughts. Bring in the good. And cling to them for dear life.

Prayer:

Lord Jesus, I thank you that I am a new creation. I thank you for giving me the ability to take thoughts captive for you. Please help me to banish the bad thoughts and dwell on the good. Please take over every aspect of my life Lord Jesus. I want you to be the captain of my thoughts. Amen.

To Dwell

> He who dwells in the shelter of the Most High
> Will abide in the shadow of the Almighty. (Psalm 91)

The more I study Psalm 91, the more it transforms my life.

When I first asked Christ to be my Savior, I was invited into his shelter. I have a standing invitation to enter. But no one is going to push me through the door.

It is up to me whether or not I "dwell" there.

The Hebrew word here translated "dwells" is *yashab*: to dwell, to remain/stay, to sit down, to have one's abode.

I think of it as living there. Staying put. Not wandering around, in and out of his shelter. I choose to remain there, where I am safe.

His shelter is my refuge and my fortress. By choosing to dwell there, by not wandering defenseless outside of the fortress's walls, I put my trust in God.

And therefore, he delivers me from the snare of the trapper and of the deadly pestilence.

I think we are all familiar with the snares of the trapper. The food court. The potluck. The annoyingly long baby shower and its comforting chocolate cupcakes.

A pestilence is an epidemic disease. Have you recently heard anyone refer to obesity as an epidemic? I have.

When we remain under God's shelter, we are protected from the snares of the trappers, and from the sickness that these snares cause us.

45

Verse 11 tells us that when we dwell in God's refuge, he will give his angels charge over us. And these angels will guard us in *all* our ways. It can be tempting to think that angels don't worry about whether or not I indulge in some chocolate cheesecake, but the angels don't guard me in *some* of my ways. They guard me in *all* of my ways. They are always here, or at least always nearby. If we remain in God's shelter, his angels will remain our protectors.

And lastly, check out verse 16. God says that he will bless us with a long life! It may be incredibly spiritual, but it is also incredibly logical: if we rely fully on God, he will guard us with his angels, keep us healthy, and reward us with long lives!

Prayer:

Almighty God, thank you for giving me a refuge to run to. Help me to remember to stay where I am safe. Prevent me from straying beyond your protective shadow. Thank you for your angels. Thank you for your protection. Thank you for this life. Help me make it a long and healthy one that will glorify you. Amen.

Music, Music, Music

> Praise Him with timbrel and dancing;
> Praise Him with stringed instruments and pipe. (Psalm 150:4)

I heard this crazy rumor that some people don't like music. If you are one of those people, there is no judgment here, and you may just want to flip to the next devotion.

Still with me? Good. Because I think music is a mightily powerful tool and I have used it every single day to help me get healthier.

First of all, music helps me want to *move*. Whether it's tapping my toe or having a dance party with the kids, moving is good for me. Movement gets the endorphins and serotonin flowing, which makes me feel better, which keeps me from overeating, which makes me feel better ...

Second, music improves my mood. Just the sound of music is empowering, even without the lyrics. This makes me feel better. And when my mood is stable, it is easier to make better food choices.

Third, I find it much more difficult to slip up when I am actively praising God. If I am singing Hallelujah with my hands in the air, it does not even occur to me to reach for a potato chip.

And lastly, music motivates me. It makes me stronger. It encourages me. A number of songs have served as my anthem throughout this journey. Please see "The Jesus Diet Soundtrack" at the end of this book. (And please let others know what songs have served as your anthems in the online version of the list.)

Here's an example. I am bowling with my extended family. There are children everywhere. The family decides to order pizza. Suddenly, there is pizza everywhere. Suddenly, I am famished. Suddenly, I can think of nothing but that pizza. Would it have been the end of the world if I had partaken? Probably not. But you see, I don't eat just one piece of pizza. It would have escalated into an abusive situation that would have led me down a trail of guilt and probably further abuse.

So this is what I did. I literally turned my back to the group and the pizza. And I began to hum "Our God" by Chris Tomlin. Does that sound a bit strange? I'll tell you, it *felt* a bit strange, antisocial even. But it worked. The craving subsided. I did not eat the pizza. It was a small victory, but it was a crucial one.

 Today, I never leave home without an anthem on my tongue. I sing my prayers and my praises, and I keep the volume turned up.

Prayer:

Lord, I thank you and praise you for the gift of music. Please help me to use this tool in service of you. Help me to live my life with my hands, my heart, and my voice lifted to you. Amen.

The Father of Lies

> Whenever he speaks a lie, he speaks from his own nature, for he is a liar and the father of lies. (John 8:44b)

Jesus spoke these words about Satan. Satan, who "prowls around like a roaring lion, seeking someone to devour" (1 Peter 5:8).

The devil is a murderer and a liar. He wants to devour you and he leads you toward your death with seductive lies. These are biblical truths.

I've been told by well-meaning believers that the devil doesn't care about me, that he's got bigger fish to fry, that he certainly doesn't care what my scale says. Not only do I think this is not true, I think it is *one of his lies*. The more people who believe this, the more people Satan can keep fat, unhappy, and less effective for Christ.

Have you ever heard any of these lies:

- Your weight is no big deal.
- This one indulgence is no big deal.
- One bite won't matter.
- You will always be fat.
- Praying about your weight is selfish.
- You deserve this food reward.
- You deserve to be fat.
- You are ugly.
- God does not love you.

If you haven't heard any of these lies, stop and thank the Lord right now. I've heard them all, over and over. And it has been a battle to shut them out. But the Bible tells us how to win that battle: Submit to God. Resist the devil and he will flee from you (James 4:7).

Give the battle to God. Submit to him in everything. Resist the devil. Resist his lies. Resist his temptations. And he will flee.

I was standing in the checkout lane. The kids were driving me nuts. There was a giant candy bar calling out to me. And a silent voice said, "Go ahead. It's only $.99. It will make you feel better. It will calm you down. You're hungry."

And I said, aloud, "In the name of Jesus, get behind me Satan!" And I felt a little bit crazy and a little bit awesome. And Satan got behind me. And God enabled me to avoid those 300 calories and that slippery slide those 300 calories would have caused.

Prayer:

Dear Jesus, thank you for beating Satan once and for all. Help me to rest in that victory. Help me to resist the enemy and make him flee from me. Protect me from temptation, Lord Jesus. Make me healthy and strong, both spiritually and physically. Amen.

All to the Glory of God

Whether, then, you eat or drink or whatever you do, do all to the glory of God. (1 Corinthians 10:31)

Paul is writing about whether to eat food that had been offered to idols. I don't mean to take this verse out of context. But I do think we can glean a powerful (not to mention poetic) principle from this verse.

If we attempt to do everything we do for the glory of God, how can we possibly go wrong? I want to glorify God. I want to make decisions that glorify God. This includes big decisions and seemingly insignificant ones.

I know that when I overeat, I am not glorifying God. I know that when I choose to self-medicate with food, I am not glorifying God.

But, when I do my best, when I seek him first, when I surrender to his will, I know that I *do* glorify him, and that is a glorious knowledge.

Prayer:

Almighty God, help me to do everything for your glory. I want to accomplish great things for you God, but I want to glorify you in all of the little things too. Please help me to consider my Creator with each step I take. Thank you, God. Amen.

Where Does Fasting Fit?

> Then I proclaimed a fast there at the river of Ahava,
> that we might humble ourselves before our God to
> seek from Him a safe journey for us, our little ones,
> and all our possessions. (Ezra 8:21)

Before fasting, discuss fasting and your unique situation with a physician.

Ezra, a foreshadowing of Christ, led Israel to spiritual reformation. And fasting was one of the tools that Ezra used. Ezra declared a fast so that the people might *humble themselves before God*. Ezra declared a fast as part of their prayer, as part of their request for a safe journey.

Please understand this: *I am not telling you to fast to lose weight.* That would not be physically healthy nor spiritually healthy. I *am* encouraging you to fast in order to grow closer to God, in order to humble yourself before him, in order to seek him.

If this fasting results in a few pounds lost, then great. If it doesn't, well that's great too. Because this fasting *will* lead to you to better spiritual health, which will lead you to better physical health.

Think you can't fast? Think again. If I can fast, anyone can. And I didn't think I could. So I asked God for help. And he enabled me to fast. I remember so clearly the first time I completed a 24-hour fast. (Yes, I had several failed attempts first.) I felt *awesome*. I felt so close to God and so clear-minded. It was an amazing experience, and truly, I wasn't even that hungry.

Remember that there is more than one way to fast. I have yet to go without coffee in the morning. When I fast, I still drink coffee and water throughout the day. But I don't eat. Others commit to a Daniel fast, during which they abstain from meat, sweets, and breads. Others fast from one particular food; they may commit to giving up sugar or coffee (I shudder to think) for a week.

Whatever you do, do it prayerfully. Ask God how he would have you fast. Then commit your fast to him and ask him to reveal himself and his will to you as you fast.

Prayer:

Heavenly Father, thank you for the gift of fasting. Thank you for the example of Ezra. If you want me to fast, please make that clear to me. Please direct my steps and enable me to accomplish your will for my life. I want to focus on you. I want to seek you. I want to be close to you. Amen.

Complacency

> So the LORD said to Joshua, "Rise up! Why is it that
> you have fallen on your face? ... Rise up! Consecrate
> the people and say, 'Consecrate yourselves for
> tomorrow, for thus the LORD, the God of Israel, has
> said, "There are things under the ban in your midst, O
> Israel. You cannot stand before your enemies until
> you have removed the things under the ban from your
> midst."'" (Joshua 7:10, 13)

When I started to get healthier, I started to lose weight and I started to feel *a lot* better. So I thought, "Hey, good job Robin, you can ease up now, right?" Wrong. So very wrong.

The Israelites were on a roll. Battle after battle, God delivered them to victory. I wonder if they got so used to the miracles that they forgot who was responsible for them.

I wonder if they got cocky. I wonder if they became complacent.

I have slipped. I have had some embarrassing slips, actually. I won't tell you how embarrassing. But then I found myself, face down like Joshua, wondering what on earth had gone wrong.

Duh. I had forgotten who was responsible for the miracles. I had let other priorities creep in. I had gotten cocky, complacent. I had forgotten that I was consecrated. And I didn't stand a chance against unhealthy foods until I got my act together with God.

I had to come back to the basics. I had to remember what mattered. I had to get up and get my house in order.

Prayer:

Lord, I thank you for the success that I've had on this journey toward health. I thank you for the success that I am yet to have. Please protect me from complacency. Please don't ever let me take you or any of your miracles for granted. Please keep me strong so that I can stand before the enemy and not fall. Amen.

Many Counselors

> Without consultation, plans are frustrated,
> But with many counselors they succeed. (Proverbs 15:22)

(1) I've read a plethora of diet books, and not one of them has ever said, "It is really important that you do this alone."

The Holy Spirit may be the only *teacher* we need, but the Bible is clear that getting wise advice from wise people is also a wise idea.

(2) I asked God to send me people to help me and he did. I surrounded myself with people who believed in me, who cared about me, and who wanted to see me succeed. But it wasn't easy. The team God assembled for me didn't look a lot like the one I had imagined for myself.

(3) Be warned that some people are uncomfortable with change. Some people will work against change without even realizing it. Someone who really does love you may not understand what you're going through, or may not believe that "this time will be different," or may be too busy working through their own issues to help you with yours.

(4) So ask God to assemble a team of counselors for you. Ask God to build you a dream team. Maybe you need a personal trainer. Maybe you can find an online friend going through a similar transformation. Your team might be made up of your pastor, your doctor, and your kid's piano teacher. Who knows?

(5) But the point is, don't go it alone. There is power in encouragement from others. There is power in accountability. Iron sharpens iron, right? (Proverbs 27:17) So do your best to surround yourself with iron.

And let God deal with the naysayers. You've got bigger fish to fry, er, I mean, broil.

Prayer:

Almighty God, thank you for giving us the gift of fellowship and friendship. Please fill my life with people who will make me stronger for you. Please send me friends and counselors who will help me grow closer to you. Amen.

Love One Another

> This is My commandment, that you love one another, just as I have loved you. (John 15:12)

Don't Totally Agree

My weight was preventing me from actively loving others.

I would see a sister crying, and I would want to wrap my arms around her, but I was so uncomfortable with my own body that I didn't want to get close to her.

My friend needed help moving to a fifth story apartment, but I knew if I tried to help, I would have a heart attack on my first trip up the stairs.

What if someone's life was in danger? Would I even be *able* to lay down my life for a friend? Or would I be stuck on the couch like a beetle trying to roll over?

It became painfully apparent to me that in order to serve God fully, I had to be in better physical shape. It is one thing to have limitations—we all have these. It is quite another thing to enforce limitations on oneself, and that is what I was doing. I was essentially crippling myself.

When I make smart decisions about my health, I become better equipped to serve God, to serve his Kingdom, and to love others. It's that simple.

Prayer:

Lord Jesus, thank you for this commandment. Please help me to follow it. Please help me to love my brothers and sisters the way you want me to love them. Please get rid of anything standing in the way of that happening. Thank you, Lord Jesus. Amen.

I Want to Look Good for My God

> and keep a good conscience so that in the thing in which you are slandered, those who revile your good behavior in Christ will be put to shame. (1 Peter 3:16)

Sue was a gifted youth ministry leader. She led countless young people to the Lord and had a positive impact on hundreds of lives.

And Sue was overweight. So her naysayers hissed "glutton" at her. Heartbreaking, right? Absolutely. Unfair, right? Absolutely. Sue did not deserve that.

 But whether we like it or not, our physical bodies are part of our testimonies. If I want to have a strong testimony, I need to have my act together. This includes my physical health.

 Now, of course I'm not saying that God can't or won't use a person who is overweight. That would be ridiculous. What I am saying is that I want to look good for my God. I may be the only glimpse of Christ a person sees on a given day. I want that glimpse to be of a healthy, confident, attractive person who looks happy in her own skin.

Those naysayers will probably always be able to come up with something heartbreaking to say, but I don't want to hand them the ammunition.

Prayer:

God Almighty, thank you for using me even though I am a flawed and broken person. Please help me to look good for you. Please help me to shine with health and confidence so that my testimony can be more complete. Amen.

We Will Overcome

These things I have spoken to you, so that in Me you may have peace. In the world you have tribulation, but take courage; I have overcome the world. (John 16:33)

A while ago, my best friend convinced me to go to a Jeremy Camp concert. It's hard to imagine now, but back then, I didn't know Jeremy or his music from a hole in the wall. Then, due to no fault of her own, my friend couldn't go.

It was truly one of those days. Everything had gone wrong and I was *grumpy*. I wasn't fit to be around people, let alone at a worship gathering, but there I was, in a frump. Angry. Annoyed.

Things got better when Jeremy hit the stage. Obviously. I listened to his lyrics and the ice around my heart melted. Over the next hour, I fell in love with Jeremy and his music. Then, at the end of the concert, Jeremy sang a song I'd never heard before: "Overcome."

The song draws on Revelation 12:11:

And they overcame him because of the blood of the Lamb and because of the word of their testimony, and they did not love their life even when faced with death.

As the fans belted out the lyrics, Jeremy asked us to join hands with our neighbors and lift our hands to the heavens. I felt the New Englander within me stiffen at the suggestion of physical contact, and I mustn't have been the only one, because Jeremy quickly quipped, "Stop complaining; you're just practicing for heaven."

So I did as I was told. Don't want to be unprepared when I get to heaven after all. I joined hands with strangers and I lifted my tired, grumpy arms toward the ceiling, and I began to sing along with the song I was hearing for the first time. And something happened. The tears began to roll down my cheeks.

I had only lost about 15 pounds at the time. But there in that moment, I was told loud and clear, that I would definitely overcome my struggle with overeating. It may have been the most spiritually powerful moment of my entire life. (It's so hard to measure these things.) I cried and cried. And I sang and sang. And God told me that I would indeed overcome, by the blood of the Lamb, by the word of my testimony. I would overcome because Jesus had overcome.

I will overcome. Maybe in this lifetime. Maybe not. Does it matter? Jesus has promised us, right there in red and white. Take heart. He has overcome this world and all its struggles, and therefore: we will overcome this world too.

Prayer:

Lord Jesus, I take heart! I know that you have overcome this world! I thank you and praise you for overcoming and I ask you to help me do the same. I want nothing to stand in my way. I want nothing to stand between me and you. Thank you, Lord Jesus for enabling me to overcome my eating issues! Amen.

Finish Strong

I have fought the good fight, I have finished the course, I have kept the faith; (2 Timothy 4:7)

Paul sensed that he would soon to be going home to his Father, and he wrote these words to his dear friend Timothy.

How much I want to be able to say these same words when I sense my end is near. How much I don't want to find myself saying, "I didn't really fight very hard. There is so much I wish I'd done differently. I wish that I had kept the faith."

Guess which of those first 50 pounds took me the longest to lose.

The fiftieth.

I had set this goal of losing 50 pounds, and when I got to the brink, I panicked. I don't know why I panicked, but I did. I slipped. I backslid. I got lazy. I was scared to lose that last pound. What on earth?

I had to beg God to get me back on track. I had to take all of my own advice all over again; I had to re-surrender all over again. But I did. And God was faithful. And I know that if I let him, he will continue to deliver me from my destructive relationship with food. If I let him, he will enable me, through the amazing, loving, supernatural power of the Holy Spirit, to finish this fight strong, to keep the faith.

Prayer:

Heavenly Father, thank you for this journey. Thank you for getting me off to such a good start. I praise you for my successes. I praise you for my failures. Please help me to fight the good fight. Please help me to finish the course. Please help me to keep the faith. I want to be strong until the end for you, Father. Thank you! Amen.

The Jesus Diet Soundtrack

"Draw the Line" by Disciple

"My Own Worst Enemy" by Casting Crowns

"Voice of Truth" by Casting Crowns

"Killa" by Lecrae

"Walkin' on Water" by Lecrae

"Divine Intervention" by Lecrae

"New Creation" by Leeland

"So Long Self" by MercyMe

"Beautiful" by MercyMe

"Overcome" by Jeremy Camp

"Your Grace Is Enough" by Matt Maher

"No Chains on Me" by Chris Tomlin

"Our God" by Chris Tomlin

"The Time Is Now" by Phil Wickham

"Remind Me Who I Am" by Jason Gray

"The End of Me" by Jason Gray

72348539R00039

Made in the USA
Columbia, SC
30 August 2019